IN SEARCH OF ST. JAMES:
CORNWALL TO COMPOSTELA

James Matamoros, defeater of the Moors.

IN SEARCH OF ST. JAMES: CORNWALL TO COMPOSTELA
The story of a pilgrimage

ADA ALVEY

With all good wishes
Ada Alvey
September 1989.

First published 1989
© A. Alvey 1989

ISBN 1–85022–045–X p/b
ISBN 1–85022–050–6 h/b

Published by *Dyllansow Truran*
Cornish Publications
Trewolsta, Trewirgie, Redruth, Cornwall

Production Consultant Anthony Wheaton, Tedburn St Mary, Devon, UK.
0647 61 329

Printed by Bookcraft Ltd., Midsomer Norton, Somerset, UK.

DEDICATION

To my sister Enid Alvey for her encouragement and
interest from the beginning.

ACKNOWLEDGEMENTS

I wish to express my gratitude to H.L. Douch and Angela Broome for their untiring and generous support given to me, when I was researching in the library of the Royal Institution of Cornwall. Without their help, my book would be but a shadow of its present form.

My travelling companion was the Hon. Mrs Pat Burke of Broadclyst, Devon, a very erudite person who already knew Santiago, and throughout the Pilgrimage helped me to anticipate the next step in the journey. When the celebrations were in full swing, she helped me to appreciate their significance. I owe her a big debt of gratitude.

When in Spain, travelling from Bilbao to Santiago, I was most grateful to the officials in the Tourist Offices and Information Bureaux. They were interested to learn of the study I was doing, and offered me the most beautiful and detailed brochures. I have used some of these to supplement the photographs I took.

Not only do they embellish the book, but I hope they may help to inspire many future Pilgrims to Santiago della Compostela.

The endpapers show the mediaeval representation of the annunciation of Christ's birth to the shepherds, painted on the ceiling of the Pantheon in the Basilica of San Isidoro.

PREFACE

For some years I have been researching into pilgrimages to Santiago de Compostela by Cornish men and women in mediaeval times.

To me, it was the story of two environments, rather like Dickens' "Tale of Two Cities", but so much wider in scope and deeper in feeling. The golden cord connecting them was the Pilgrims' Way from Cornwall, across the Bay of Biscay, and over mountains and scorching plains to a small city in Galicia, where the Cornish and Spanish Celts would meet.

I planned to show how these regions interacted; how the pilgrimages left their mark on Cornwall and on Spain, and what must have been the effect on the pilgrims themselves.

For a pilgrimage was a profound experience: as an encounter with the unknown, it was an enrichment of life; new experiences and learning made life richer; rising to a great challenge gave satisfaction; the comradeship of fellow pilgrims gave confidence; and the great reward of reaching their goal must have strengthened their religious faith, providing memories which would have lasted a life-time.

INTRODUCTION

Camino de Santiago (The Way To Santiago)

I, Peregrina of the 20th century, set off in July 1983 to visit Santiago della Compostela, hoping to arrive in time to celebrate the Feast of St. James on July 25th.

My ancestors on my father's side lived in the Basque country, while my mother's are Cornish – a truly Celtic background. I was anxious to follow the Pilgrims' Way trodden by Cornish pilgrims in mediaeval times, and who better to do it?

Mediaeval Pieta from Tywardreath Priory

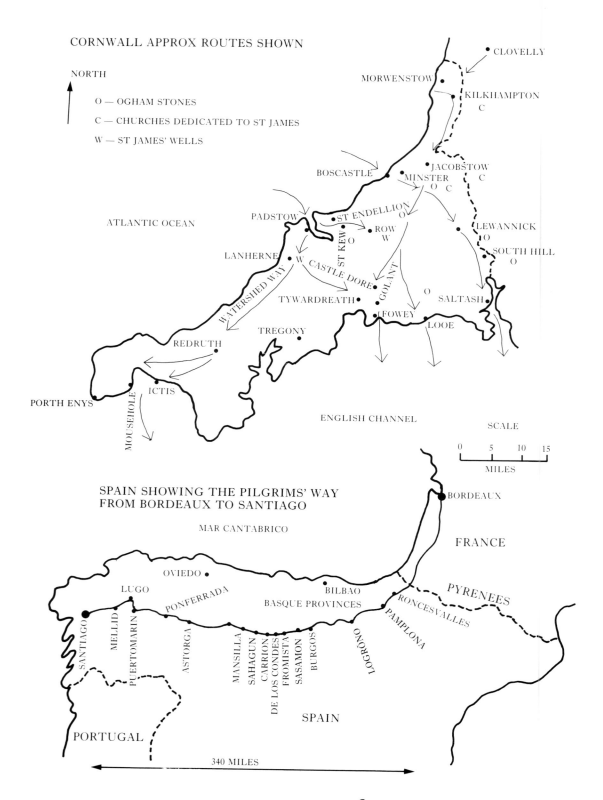

CORNWALL APPROX ROUTES SHOWN

NORTH

O — OGHAM STONES

C — CHURCHES DEDICATED TO ST JAMES

W — ST JAMES' WELLS

CLOVELLY

MORWENSTOW

KILKHAMPTON
C

BOSCASTLE

JACOBSTOW
C

MINSTER
O C

ATLANTIC OCEAN

PADSTOW

ST ENDELLION
O

ROW
W

LEWANNICK
O

SOUTH HILL
O

LANHERNE

W

CASTLE DORE

ST KEW
O

GOLANT

WATERSHED WAY

TYWARDREATH

O

SALTASH

FOWEY

REDRUTH

TREGONY

LOOE

PORTH ENYS

ICTIS

MOUSEHOLE

ENGLISH CHANNEL

SCALE

0   5   10   15

MILES

BORDEAUX

SPAIN SHOWING THE PILGRIMS' WAY
FROM BORDEAUX TO SANTIAGO

MAR CANTABRICO

FRANCE

OVIEDO

PYRENEES

LUGO

PONFERRADA

BILBAO

BASQUE PROVINCES

RONCESVALLES

MELLID

SANTIAGO

PUERTOMARIN

ASTORGA

MANSILLA

SAHAGUN

CARRION
DE LOS CONDES

FROMISTA

SASAMON

BURGOS

LOGROÑO

PAMPLONA

PORTUGAL

SPAIN

340 MILES

2

IN SEARCH OF SAINT JAMES

Since early days of Christianity, pilgrimages have been undertaken to venerated sites, such as Compostela. The arduous journey was a sign of devotion and many people sought salvation with the help of the dispensations from the punishment of sin (known in the church as indulgences) which could be obtained by going on pilgrimages.

The pilgrimage was an opportunity to acquire relics, such as a splinter of the true cross, a hair of St Mary Magdalene, a drop of holy blood or other objects of piety. These were important for, if cathedrals or abbeys for example were to be built, relics had to be obtained to be housed within the walls. Knights would journey on pilgrimages to prepare themselves spiritually for dangerous missions and to give thanks for successful outcomes.

The sick and the handicapped might also become pilgrims, in the hope that they would be cured. Criminals who had committed murder or other violent crimes were sentenced to go on pilgrimage and were pardoned when they returned with a certificate from the priest. Pilgrimages of thanks might also be undertaken, in gratitude for a successful venture, or for preservation from danger.

There was also a motley array of pilgrims with unspiritual aspirations; for instance, merchants with goods to trade, artisans looking for work, minstrels, dancers, and other less savoury characters such as adventurers and thieves who preyed on their fellow pilgrims.

Some people, instead of braving the dangers and discomforts of a pilgrimage, employed a deputy, who for a fixed tariff undertook the pilgrimage.

As Chaucer tells us, Spring was the most popular time to begin a pilgrimage. Weatherwise, the snows were receding on the high land, the days were getting longer, and it was good to reach one's goal at a great festival. But the most popular day to celebrate a visit to Compostela was, and is, St. James' Day, July 25th.

Santiago de Compostela

The fame of Santiago de Compostela as a place of pilgrimage grew from the 9th century onwards, and was at its height in the 11th century. Originally, the three great cities of Christian pilgrimage were Jerusalem, Rome and Santiago de Compostela, and the indulgences received by pilgrims to Santiago were considered to be worth half those gained from Jerusalem. But the value increased, until by the time of the Crusades the dispensations were of equal value.

St. James the Great was the brother of St. John and a son of Zebedee; he witnessed the Transfiguration and the Agony in the Garden of Gethsemane and was beheaded by King Herod Agrippa. It was claimed from the 7th century onwards that St. James had preached the gospel in Spain. and that after his death his body was brought to Spain. About 810 AD, Theodomir, Bishop of Iris Flavia (Padron) in Galicia, found in a tomb on the site of Compostela three bodies, believed to be James the Great and two of his disciples. The Bishop and King Alfonso II of Asturias informed Pope Leo III and Charlemagne. This was the time of the Moorish occupation of Spain, and the defeat of the Moors at Poitiers 732 and another victory 718 at Cavadonga had given hope that they would eventually be expelled from Europe. The miraculous discovery of St. James' body came just at the right time to inspire the Christians to drive the Moors backward to the south. In a legendary battle against the Moors in 844 a knight in armour on a horse, with a red-crossed white standard, appeared and routed the enemy; he was immediately identified as St. James, who then acquired the name of "Matamore" or "Moor Slayer".

Over the necropolis where the body had been found, rose the town of Santiago de Compostela, the church and monastery being built by Alfonso the Chaste. So began the crowds of pilgrims travelling across Europe to venerate the shrine. At the time of the Crusades, when Jerusalem had been attacked by the Saracens, pilgrims could not visit the Holy Land, so Santiago became the most important centre of pilgrimage. Some of Santiago's more famous pilgrims were St. Francis of Assisi, St. Bridgid of Sweden, John of Gaunt, and Katharine of Aragon, before she married Prince Arthur.

Pilgrims were protected by the Knights of Santiago, who patrolled the Moorish frontier. Pilgrims carried a pilgrim's staff and wore the distinguishing badge of an escallop shell or a cockle shell on the cloak or hat. This symbol derives from the legend that when the relics of St. James were being conveyed from Jerusalem to Spain in a marble ship, the horse of a Portuguese knight took fright and plunged into the sea, taking his rider with him. When the knight was rescued, his clothing was covered with scallop shells.

At the height of the era of pilgrimages, from Burgos, along the 340 miles of the Pilgrims' Way, there were stopping places for prayer, sleep and sustenance, about every two miles, in the form of cathedrals, monasteries, churches, hospices and hospitals. Now, many of these buildings have crumbled away and the houses around them have been abandoned. Parts of the Pilgrims' Way have become overgrown and impossible to follow. But there is still a succession of interesting buildings, with breathtakingly beautiful sculptures, carving, gold ornaments and stained glass.

The Celtic missionaries of the 5th and 6th centuries, crossed the Celtic Sea to the south-west peninsula, which today, through its length and breadth, carries the names of these saints in the names of towns, villages and holy wells. Today, visitors to Cornwall are amazed to see parish churches dedicated to Celtic saints they have never even heard of. These men and women set up a simple hut beside a spring of fresh water. Some lived out their lives in the spot they chose, others travelled further afield, like St. Beatus, who reached Switzerland and lived in a natural cave by Lake Thun, still reached by visitors along a pilgrim's path. Others, remaining in Cornwall, by their piety, scholarship and leadership, had a profound influence on the people among whom they lived. How rich these names, and how musically they trip off the tongue; St. Nectan, St. Piran, St. Petroc, St. Winwalloe, St. Keyne, St. Finnbarrus.

In later times, those who could not manage the arduous and expensive foreign crusades made local pilgrimages to holy shrines at St. Michael's Mount, Bodmin and St. Germans, the first being the most popular. Henry Marshall, Bishop of Exeter, in 1206, granted several advowsons to the monastery of the Mount, so that hospitality could be provided for pilgrims. Many pilgrims from outside Cornwall, for instance from Ireland and Wales, visited these shrines.

Now to the pilgrims who travelled further afield. These are the pilgrims with whom these pages are principally concerned. To these pilgrims, Cornwall became a bridge for those from Ireland and Wales, wishing to avoid the often stormy passage around Lands End.

Many combined two pilgrimages; first to St. Michael's Mount and then sailing on probably to Bordeaux to continue on foot to Santiago de Compostela. The tracks along the north coast from Boscastle, Harlyn Bay or the Camel estuary further north had already been marked out in the distant past by Bronze and Iron age men, who traded in metals. The tracks kept to the rugged, windswept moor to avoid the forests filling the valleys. The pilgrims crossing Cornwall and the Cornish people themselves, used ports on the south coast. Strange as it seems

Drying nets, Mousehole. Has it really changed very much, when viewed against the sun?

to us today, at one time the two most important ports transporting pilgrims to Spain were Saltash and Mousehole.

One important stream of traffic began at Clovelly, then south into Cornwall. Holy wells and Ogham stones made very good signposts.

The route across north Cornwall from west to east shows many connections with St. James. There was a chapel dedicated to St. James at Boscastle;

7

Botrescastell. A chapel of Seynt James in the seyd towne, distant from the parysh church there iij quarters of a myle. the Parson of Mynster and his predecessors have alwaies accustomed to paye to the prest in the chappell yerely iiij ll (Chantries Commission Feb 4 37 Henry VIII 1545).

William of Worcester reports that

Sancta Matheriana virgo jacet in ecclesia parochiae de Mynstre per dimidium miliare de Botreaux Castelle, et per iii miliaria de Camelford: fecit unum miraculum de quaem homine extra sensum ac una muliere et quadam puella in festa Sancti Jacobi, uno anno preterito, et eius festum agitur circa 9 diem Aprilis.

William Decimarius, Prior of Minster Priory, succeeded July 8, 1349. Yearly value of his receipts:-

fr. Minster Church – 10 marks and 7½d.
fr. the Chapel at Botreaux Castle 8 mks and 9½d.

The Priory ceased to exist in 1407. The Fair was held on the Festival of St. James, July 25th.

An ancient road connects Boscastle with Jacobstow and then on to Kilkhampton. The church at Jacobstow belonged to the Manor of Penhallem. In 1270 it was named as "the Church of St. James of Penhallym". A holy well of St. James is situated on a hill in the parish owned by Mr. Jack Stephens of Trefrida. It is in a one-acre field of wooded, marshy land. It is now derelict.

St. James the Great is also the patron saint of the fine church at Kilkhampton. The original dedication was to St. Kea. The change may have come about when FitzHamon, the great Earl of Gloucester, who was given this Manor, handed over the churches on his Cornish fiefs to the Priory of St. James at Bristol, daughter house of the Abbey of Tewkesbury. There is an added reason

In Search of St. James

Statue of St. James, Kilkampton Church. He has certainly stood up to the ravages of the Cornish weather exceedingly well.

St. James' well at Ball, which supplied Lanherne Convent with water.

Lanherne Convent. Statue of St. James (above) and a scallop shell on the gate.

that Kilkhampton with Morwenstow lay on the route between Wales and Santiago de Compostela.

A splendid statue of St. James looks out from his niche in the wall of the church. There is no mistaking his identity. He stands there wearing his broad-brimmed hat bearing a scallop shell, and a scrip and wallet by his side. He boldly holds his pilgrim's staff, and looks as if he is ready to start out on a pilgrimage to Spain.

At Morwenstow, the neighbouring church sheltering in a valley from winter's Atlantic gales, there were crosses to St. John and St. James, which have now disappeared.

At St. Breward, near the hamlet of Chapel, is Chapel Farm Well. The water was good and had a wide reputation for healing sore eyes. By 1881, miners had drained the water, and the well since then has been dry. The structure is tottering, but it still retains its ancient cover. Oliver's Monasticon states that there were in the parish of St. Breward in 1442, chapels dedicated to St. Michael and St. James. Even today the foundations of the ancient St. James' Chapel can be seen by the well. St. Michael and St. James have been associated together in Cornwall; wells close together, or side by side in stained glass windows, showing that pilgrimages to the Mount and to Santiago were often closely linked.

Many chapels of St. James in Cornwall were built along the pilgrim routes, often associated with hospices nearby, used by pilgrims for rest and refreshment. Lanherne Convent is a splendid example. There can be no doubt of its importance to pilgrims. High on the front wall, above the entrance, stands St. James, and on the iron gates and on the down-pipes from the launder, are scallop shells.

But many of the buildings have lost their identity and have been difficult to discover and identify. Fowey, such an important gathering point for pilgrims about to embark for Spain, has a most interesting house, historically and architecturally, no. 9 South Street. It was thought to be a priests' house, used by monks who served

No. 9, South Street, Fowey. This is almost certainly the house where pilgrims stayed while waiting for a ship to take them to Spain.

the church and St. Catherine's chapel. They came from Tywardreath Priory, five miles away. But a more likely theory is that it was used as a pilgrim's hospice. The building is at least 500 years old, so could have been used when pilgrimages were a way of life.

Of some chapels and hospices, there is little or no trace. St. Rumon's chapel stood on the site of the library, below the railway station in Redruth. Here St. James' pilgrims made a stopping place on their journey to the south coast. Pieces of broken masonry can still be found.

12

In Search of St. James

A chapel dedicated to St. James stood at the end of Tregony Bridge. Tregony was the first town to be built on the River Fal, even before Penryn, so it was a town of some importance. Now, alas, the site of the chapel lies under a thick layer of mud, as the river gradually silted up. Tregony's Feast Day, on which a Fair was held, was July 25, St. James' Day.

The pilgrims who travelled across the Cornish peninsula, from Ireland and South Wales, crossed the Bristol Channel and landed at Clovelly, Boscastle, Harlyn Bay and the Camel Estuary. It was not an easy land journey from the west to east coast; the roads were bad and the weather over the moors was often windy and wet. The pilgrims safeguarded themselves from thieves by forming themselves into bands, and travelling in stages from chapel to hospice and so on. As they travelled, they passed ancient symbols of the earliest Christianity in Cornwall, the wayside stone crosses. These, together with Ogham stones served as sign posts, although the reason for their erection had nothing to do with pilgrimages.

During the Dark Ages for which there is a dearth of recorded history, some information comes to us from written words. These were carved in often crude and mis-spelt lettering in Ogham script, a form of shorthand, cut on the edges of memorial stones. The letters were cut where two faces of the stone met, as shown below. Most date from the 5th to the 7th centuries, spreading from Ireland to S Wales, Cornwall and beyond, at a time when there were waves of Irish invasions, following the end of Roman provincial government.

A O U E I H D C Q B L F S N M G NG Z R K

Three hundred and fifteen inscriptions are known in Ireland, and forty-eight in Southern Britain, six of which are in Cornwall, all in the area of the Camel estuary.

The inscribed stone near Slaughter Bridge, Minster, now almost lost in the river bank.

One of the Cornish inscribed stones is in St. Kew parish church, where there is only a fragment with the name Justi (Justus). Near Roscarrack, St. Endellion, is a stone with the complete inscription "Brocagni hic iacit Nadotti filius" (Here lies Brocagnus, son of Nadottus); near Slaughter Bridge, Minster, partially obscured by the river bank, tree branches and brambles, is a stone to commemorate Latinus. The stone is wedged at a peculiar angle and is difficult to photograph. The instription, still plainly legible, reads "Latini [h]ic jacit filius Maceri". (Here lies Latinus, son of Macarus).

Nearby was believed to have been fought the battle between Arthur and his nephew Mordred, in which Arthur was killed, and his body lay here in the Valley of Worthvale for three days before being carried to Glastonbury.

The village of Lewannick has two Oghams, one in the church and one in the churchyard. At St. Sampson's church, South Hill, a stone was discovered in 1891.

It was customary to set up these stones in isolation and

not in churchyards, often on the roadside in the Roman manner. So they became signposts to pilgrims and traders alike. These people spoke Goedelic. The ancient route across the Cornish peninsula from Padstow to Fowey has three stones, including the Castle Dore stone.

The pilgrims also visited shrines in Cornwall: St. Germans, St. Petroc at Bodmin and at St. Michael's Mount. But many travelled further afield. They followed the routes of St. James' chapels and wells, guided by Ogham stones, and given shelter and food in monasteries and priories. there is evidence of provision for pilgrims; for instance, in 1206, Henry Marshall, Bishop of Exeter was granted certain advowsons to the monastery on the Mount, to provide hospitality for pilgrims. Tywardreath Priory was a hospice for pilgrims on their way to Fowey.

Following the high ridge from north Cornwall to the Mount, the pilgrims continued their journey by ship, across the Bay of Biscay to Bordeaux, or Bilbao and into Spain. Cornish pilgrims in thousands travelled these routes. As we have seen, Saltash and Mousehole were the most important ports for ships taking pilgrims to Santiago, but many other creeks and inlets provided ships for the hazardous and uncomfortable sea voyage. It is difficult to imagine a tiny place such as Cargreen on the River Tamar, sending ships with pilgrims to Spain.

Cornish clergy had to obtain leave of absence from the bishop. Usually the destination, e.g. Jerusalem, Compostela or Rome, was stated, but there were exceptions. For instance Philip. Prior of Minster, in 1311, received a general permission to go "ad partes. . . .transmarinas". In 1330, the Rector of St. Erme visited Rome and then went on to Santiago de Compostela.

Laymen also went on pilgrimage. Otho de Bodrugan in 1324 was unable to attend Parliament, because with Ralph de Bello Prato (Beaupre), he was on pilgrimage to Compostela.

To combat smuggling and piracy, captains had to

obtain a licence to carry pilgrims. An indenture or contract, signed at Looe in 1395, was drawn up between the Crown and the owner of a ship, concerning service in Richard II's expedition to Ireland. As his reward, the master of the Katerine was granted a licence to carry in his own vessel from Looe, 60 pilgrims to Spain, to make their devotions at the shrine of St. James. But three pestilences, in 1349, 1361 and 1381 put an end to Looe's brief mediaeval glory.

The earlier name of Mousehole was Porth Enys (the port near the islet). Ships from Mount's Bay took pilgrims, who had obtained lodging, food and rest at Madron on Alverton Manor, provided by the Knights Templars, to Oléron and Bordeaux from where they proceeded by land.

The entries in Bishop Grandison's Register show that many pilgrims made the trip to Santiago in spite of the terrible conditions on the ships. Q quotes a mediaeval poet :-

Men may leave all gamys,
That saylen to St. Jamys.

(N.B. 'Q' was the pen name of the author, Sir Arthur Quiller Couch)

Conditions on board are also described.

Before midnight, the pilgrim will be coughing and groaning, lying across the ship's boat, and refusing all food. Warm Malvesy wine is all they will cry for. Then the Master will make a tour of the ship to see that all is well, whilst the passengers lie about in their clothes. Woe betide him who goes to bed near the ship's pump, for a man were as good as dead as smell thereof the stynke.

In Search of St. James

The following are some records of pilgrim sailings from Fowey:

1332 Vicar of Fowey
1367 John Colf, Master of the *Nicholas* of Fowey, given permission to go with his mariners on this pilgrimage.
1394 The barge *George*, Master Richard Robyn, took 60 closely packed pilgrims.
1414 John Russell, not averse to piracy, took 50 pilgrims to Spain.
1433 Pilgrim sailings were particularly popular. Licences were granted to Thomas Gerard (*Julien*), John Nicoll (*Cok John*), Philip Mayow (*Barry*), Ralph Wythyall (*Mary*).
1453 *Mary* still plying, also Thomas Tregyn.

In time the uncomfortable and dangerous voyage was over and the pilgrims were again on terra firma. Many had taken the trade route to Bordeaux; others would sail direct to a port on the north coast of Spain. But in all probability they would meet en route or at their destination.

They would be wearing a kind of pilgrim's uniform; a grey cape or cowl, fastened by a broad belt, a broad-brimmed hat, pilgrim's staff with a device at the tip, and a gourd or water bottle fastened near the top and a scrip or sack. On their feet they would wear Jacobean sandals, which would be put to the test on the rough Spanish roads. A beard would be grown.

Let us start with our Cornish pilgrims from Bordeaux and travel south towards the Pyrenees. If they are aiming to reach Santiago in time to celebrate St. James' Day, it will be summer time and the hazards of these mountain ranges will not be as severe as in winter. Some pilgrims travelled no farther; the privations put too much strain on them, or brigands robbed them of what little wealth they were carrying. Many of the little churchyards by the way marked the end of a journey of hope never to be fulfilled.

In Search of St. James

The Roncesvalles Pass was the usual gateway into Spain. It is the legendary site of the death of Roland, where Oliver ambushed Roland, the favourite of Charlemagne; when Roland blew the horn Charlemagne gave him, it was too late. (A pilgrimage was invented for Charlemagne to add to his fame and help his image.)

I will now describe how I travelled this route myself in July 1983, to arrive at Santiago on St James' Eve, not on foot alas, but visiting the same cathedrals, churches, hospices and monasteries as the mediaeval pilgrims. Our journey was by coach, our principal guide Dean Gilbert Thurlow; an excellent leader who was eager to share his wealth of information and whose enthusiasm and good humour acted like a tonic to us all.

From the Pass of Roncesvalles to Santiago is 350 miles. The pilgrims reckoned on completing the journey in 13 full days, which meant 27 miles a day. In the words of a children's rhyme:

> Out of France and into Spain
> Over the hills and back again.

Though we used this route, we did not start in the mountainous section of the Great Road, one of the mostly highly organised of all mediaeval routes, for we flew to Bilbao and joined the Great Road at Burgos. In the early middle ages, few travellers attempted to reach Compostela through the Basque country, because the people here did not welcome strangers, their language was outlandish, and they owed no allegiance to the Kings of the Franks or the Princes of the Peninsula. (I thought of that when I was advised in Santiago on the Feast Day, to avoid a certain square on the way to my hotel, because the police were trying to break up a Basque Separatist Demonstration with rubber bullets.)

So let us follow the mediaeval pilgrim through the Pyrenees, where he reached Spanish soil at Roncesvalles, and started on the Navarre road. At first, the scenery

One of the pilgrim crosses
which marks the way.

would be very different from the green fields and trees he
had left behind; the green becomes yellow and a sun-
baked plain will stretch far away to the mountains on the
horizon.

The collegiate church of Roncesvalles dates from the
13th century and was a key landmark for the pilgrims, as
was the impressive Pilgrim Cross. The following of
routes guided by Ogham stones is past; now the roadside
crosses beckon the pilgrims on.

The church is of French Gothic style. The Romanesque

chapel of Santiago has a wooden image covered in silver, which is venerated by the pilgrims.

So, on to Pamplona with its ancient walls. The oldest church is that of San Cernin, which dates from the 13th century. Several hostels were built here, the chief one being that of San Miguel.

At Puente le Reina, the routes from Paris and Arles meet. 200m before arriving here, and just off the road, is the polygonal church of Eunate, built in the 12th century. It looks strange with the cloister around the walls. A compelling statue of St. James depicts him as a strong and purposeful pilgrim.

Burgos is reached by two routes taken by pilgrims, one from Bayonne, one from Najera. The main route enters the province from Santo Domingo de la Calzada. It passes through several villages, along a gorge and in view of the impressive Oca hills.

San Juan de Ortega is a hamlet which commemorates the saint who, with Santo Domingo de la Calzada, was one of the great architects of the Road. San Juan de Ortega still boasts the fine church which this saint built in the 12th century.

Burgos, the ancient capital of Castile and Leon, looks and feels like a capital city. What gateway could be more majestic than that of Santa Maria!

The chief monument is the Cathedral. It makes its presence felt throughout the city. Both inside and outside, it is exceptional in its beauty. It was begun in 1221 and is a superb masterpiece of simple 13th century Gothic. By contrast, the 13th century spires by Hans of Cologne, are typically German and strongly resemble the spires of the Dom in Cologne, which were added in the 19th century but to the mediaeval designs. In each case, the spires are so lofty that satisfactory photography from ground level is impossible.

Building continued with the amazing star-patterned vaulted roofs of the Constable chapel, other chapels, and finally the central tower, completed in 1568.

Inside, there is so much of beauty and interest, that one is unable to fully appreciate everything. Standing beneath the transept, one is literally showered with flowing light from the lofty windows. Rodrigo Diaz de Vivar, "El Cid Campeador", lies here beside his wife Ximena. He is Spain's greatest hero. He played a large part in driving out the Moors (although it is often conveniently forgotten that as a mercenary, he sometimes fought on the other side). As defender of his country, he is allied with St. James, who, so it is said, appeared at a critical time in the struggle, and earned the title Santiago Matamoros.

The screen and grilles in the Choir consist of some of the finest wrought iron in Castile and Aragon. But in the *coro* itself are 103 superb stalls made of walnut, inlaid with boxwood, every one with its misericord. Did any

Monument to El Cid Campeador, León.

21

Cornish pilgrim turn up these, and wonder at them, admiring the intricate carving, each one different. You can imagine all the stalls being occupied and the music of Vivaldi or Monteverdi echoing around the walls. You feel almost imprisoned by these tiers of stalls. Did any Cornish miner wish to sing here, as he was wont to do at the bottom of Dolcoath?

All around the apse are chapels containing priceless treasures. One is the Chest of El Cid.

There are abundant records of pious foundations in Burgos to assist pilgrims. Outstanding amongst these was the Hospital del Rey (The King's Hospice) not far from the celebrated Monastery de Las Huelgas, both founded by Alfonso VIII.

57 km from Burgos is the monastery of San Domingo de Silos. It was founded in 919, and rebuilt in 1042. The two-storeyed cloister is considered by many the finest in Europe: "the triumphant climax of Romanesque art in Spain." It measures 33.15m by 30m. It opens onto a lawn and garden through sixty round arches. At each corner are carved New Testament scenes, for instance the south-east angle shows Christ's ascension, and Pentecost and the Holy Ghost. The capitals along the sides are carved with foliage, birds and animals; no two are alike.

Downstairs is the mediaeval museum with a wealth of filigree, paintings, monstrances and quaint treasures such as the chalice with little bells. But my favourite was part of a triptych depicting the Madonna and child in polychromed stone. She sits so calmly wearing a homely bonnet, reminding me of a fisherman's wife sitting on a step at Mousehole with her baby on her knee, or a Spanish mother, sitting on a stone overlooking the sun-baked countryside, watching the mules threshing the wheat, as I saw them.

Here in this monastery is a trained choir, one hundred strong, unsurpassed for singing Gregorian Chant. Perhaps the monks were always excellent singers. If so, the Cornish pilgrims could join them without disgrace.

Spanish landscape

Santa María del Naranco

San Miguel de Lillo

So far the countryside has been varied and interesting; woodland, patches of corn, pasture and outcrops of craggy rocks. This would be fairly familiar to the Cornish traveller, but now the landscape is beginning to spread out, sun-drenched landscapes, stretching for miles, with a far distant line of purple mountains. It is so quiet and there are no people, no traffic on the road. Just a time for digesting all we have experienced and to enjoy the wealth of colour, the bright orange tiles on the little cottages, clumps of tiny scarlet poppies by the roadside and the contrasting gold of the harvested fields and the green of the belts of trees.

This cannot have changed for hundreds of years.

My feet weren't suffering on the dusty, stony roads, like those of our mediaeval ancestors, but when they stopped to eat at a roadside bar, was it so different? I think not. I think a two-hour siesta was enjoyed then, and the simple food and drink, served with a welcoming smile, gave pleasure to all.

We were now on our way to León, our next cathedral city, a journey of about 125 miles. We were never sure how many miles we would cover in a day, because there were so many interesting diversions to tempt us away from the beaten track.

We turn right and visit Sasamón with a splendid church, Santa Maria le Real. Its portal resembles that of Burgos, with its beautifully carved figures.

In Palencia, the Road passes through Boadilla del Camino to Fromista. Here one can admire one of the most perfect Romanesque churches in Spain. It was founded in 1035 by Dona Mayor. It is difficult to decide from what angle to photograph it, but you cannot go wrong; its design and proportions are so pleasing, you will always get an attractive picture. The church is dedicated to San Martin.

Fromista had both a Moorish and a Jewish quarter, and a total of four pilgrim hospices of which the most famous was that of Palmeros, now a hostel.

The church of San Martin, Fromista, Palencia.

It was the birthplace of San Pedro González Telmo, patron saint of sailors.

We travelled 6 km south to visit San Hipolito's at Tamara. We climbed laboriously up a wooden staircase to a small gallery at the west end, and there we gazed at a strange 17th century organ perched on a single wooden pillar.

Carrión de Los Condes is an important pilgrim station. Here Santa Maria del Camino has a fine facade with a splendid carving of bulls.

The Counts of Carrión who lived here married the daughters of El Cid, and treated them badly.

On to Sahagún, where there was much suffering under the Romans and the Moors. Then later, Alphonso VI founded the great monastery, whose ruins can still be seen, and around which the town developed.

Of the nine mediaeval churches here, four still survive. San Tirso and San Lorenze both have fine brick 12th

24

The twelfth-century Mudéjar bell tower of San Lorenzo.

century Mudéjar bell towers. San Lorenzo has Moorish horseshoe arches. The Franciscan monastery of La Peregrina (the female pilgrim) has a fine doorway.

All is well as you stand facing the noble tower of San Lorenzo. You can picture in your mind the busy town around it, as the thousands of pilgrims were accommodated and served; and business being transacted. Cornish woollens were probably bartered or sold and Spanish leather carried back to Cornwall.

The many hostels and the four hospitals were always active. In 1255, a 14-day fair was held by the River Cea, and trade was booming.

But stop day-dreaming. Turn round and survey the scene. What a contrast!

Sahagún is now desolate and impoverished. Cracked tiles fall from the decaying roofs, no-one sits at the thresholds of these houses. Tattered, drunken notices, one after another, declare that the properties are "TO LET", but only the birds are interested.

This was the saddest picture I saw on the pilgrimage.

But we must press on towards León. After the walled village of Mansilla de Las Mulas, we crossed the River Esla. Here you get a fine view of the village and the surrounding wall.

We turn right and go on an exploratory journey to our next objective. The road changes to a narrow track, which twists and turns. It goes on and on, but we think we are on the right road. The people and dogs from the roadside cottages certainly look as though they take us for invaders from outer space. Perhaps the smiling optimistic nods in reply to our queries, merely mean they haven't a clue as to what we are asking, but they don't want us to be disappointed.

Then it happens. The track curves into an open space in front of a most interesting church, built in 913 by refugee Mozarabic monks from Córdoba, who used the horseshoe arch thoughout, even in the ground floor of the apses. It is the Church of S. Miguel Escalada. The exterior galley is unusual. The aisled nave was built 930. The tower is 11th century. Here are the remains of an ancient hospice.

The scenery of Palencia changes as you travel westward. Across the flat plain the roads seem endless, and the orange and yellow fields simply melt into a haze of sunny background, but gradually the oaks and the ilexes appear in valleys and crags rear themselves to form a wilder landscape. This is a rich land, ideal for rearing

So the landscape changes from Palencia to León.

Near a small village (right) the local women do their washing in the river and spread it on the grass to dry. Meanwhile, children seek relief from the blazing sun in these cool arcades.

The golden sun-baked farmlands of Palencia. Flowers, like these roses, struggle to survive.

sheep or goats. Soon we come to an important coal-mining area. The rivers teem with trout. We are now climbing higher. To our left in the thick woods of the valley, we see at intervals, the greyish brown ruinous spires and roofs of churches and hospices, now almost forgotten and lost among the trees. Some pilgrims following vague tracks through the woods, thump with their staffs on the ground, hoping to hear the reassuring ring of stone beneath their feet. It is becoming cooler now, for we are on our way to the green fields and rainy climate of Galicia. Some pilgrims must have become anxious, because high mountain passes have to be crossed, before the goal is reached.

So we travel on to León, so called from the VIIth Roman Legion quartered by by Augustus. Highland country with a rugged profile, it was the base from which the reconquest of the country sprang. It lies between green Galicia and greyish brown Castile. Life has adapted to the varying land forms. Farming villages are hidden in valleys, castles keep a watchful eye from the peaks, while soaring spires rise to heaven in the glory of God. The Cantabrian Range to the north is majestic, rising well above the tree line; it is snow-covered in winter. After the sacking by Almanzor, León recovered under Alfonso V and during the 11th century became the capital of the kingdom. Those who made the pilgrimage to Santiago spoke of León as a city "full of all delights".

León is a city of two parts, the old and the new. In the old part, familiar to the pilgrims of mediaeval times, the interesting buildings are found in the Plaza Mayor.

The Cathedral takes pride of place. The building began in 1205, a universal jewel of Gothic art. It may not equal Burgos in dramatic line, because the spires are not as lofty, but enter the door, and immediately you are bathed in a glow of glorious colour. It is a symphony of light and stone. The mediaeval glass has been preserved almost in its entirety. Everywhere is colour and light. Even the triforium was stained glass. There were windows with entwining plants, single dramatic Old Testament characters, magnificent rose windows and even in tiny remote corners, exquisite patterns, shining with all the intensity of a jewel. I was speechless. Surely no cathedral can vie with this glorious sight. Does any other cathedral have as many rose windows? León has 60 of which 3 are giant rose windows. All the slender stone columns seem to serve no other function but to frame the windows.

The Basilica of San Isidoro was built as a mausoleum

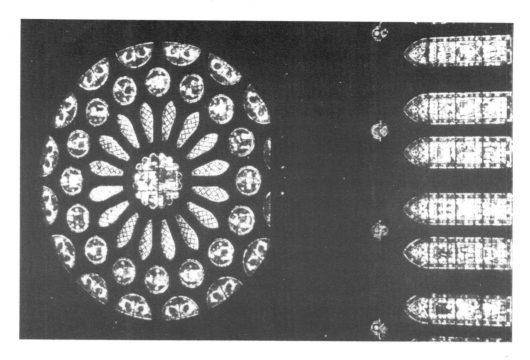

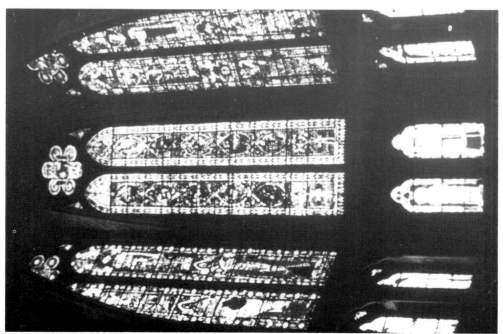

The magnificent stained glass windows of León.

for the remains of San Isidoro de Sevilla, on the orders of
Fernando I, in 1063. The body of the church is Romanesque, the upper parts Gothic and the cornice is Renais-
sance. The capitals of the Pantheon were decorated first,
with scenes from the Gospels.

A little over 30 miles west of León lies Astorga, a very
ancient city still surrounded by the remains of enormous
Roman walls 22 feet thick. They have been much
repaired following damage by Almanzor. Three cathedrals have stood here: a Romanesque building conse-

The cloisters of San Isidoro.

32

crated in 1069; a 13th century replacement of which nothing remains; and a third begun in 1471, which took a long time to complete.

Astorga is built on the side of a hill, with the cathedral in a dominant position. As you view it from the waste land covered with weeds, outside the high city walls, it looks remote and impersonal.

Astorga looks to the towering mountains where the Pilgrim's Way leads, and it leaves one with a cold and lonely feeling. It stands at the entrance to the mountain passes, so plenty of hospitals and monasteries provided a short rest for the travellers before they tackled the barren mountain passes. Francis of Assisi stayed either in the hospital of San Juan or that of San Roque.

We go now to the bare rugged mountains of León, over the Manzanal Pass, where there is a 12th century pilgrim hospice 3,750 feet up. Here live the Maragato, possibly the last of the Berbers who came with the Moors. They are a strange people, who like to keep themselves to themselves. They have family rituals, solemn weddings and some odd customs; for instance they carry their dead in coffins to their burial place by night. They wear attractive regional costumes.

We pass Ponferrada, so named because of its iron-clad bridge, built 1082–86, by order of the Bishop of Astorga. Before this, the pilgrims used a ferry, to cross the River Boeza further north.

Now the weather is changing. No longer are the skies cloudless and the sun beating down relentlessly the whole day long, so that we sit in the shade and eat with relish the giant peaches bought at the village shop.

Now we are reminded of home, as all Cornish and Irish pilgrims must have so long ago. Cloudy skies, a hint of rain and one day in the mountains an absolute deluge. But luckily it doesn't last long.

We cross the Bierzo valley and bypass Villafranca. We climb up the Piedrafita Pass, 3638 feet, and now make a detour from the old Pilgrim Road to visit Lugo.

The mighty Roman walls of Lugo (above) and the Puerto de Santiago (the Santiago gate).

At Lugo, pilgrims who crossed the Piedrafita Pass, as we did, met those who came from Oviedo.

We returned from Santiago via Oviedo, so it would be a good idea to consider that town here and now. It was almost completely destroyed during the Civil War, but overlooking the rebuilt Oviedo are two remarkable churches, with a unique style of architecture, only found in Asturias; Santa Maria del Naranco and San Miguel de Lillo.

Lugo is completely circled by an undamaged Roman wall built of slate, 20 feet thick and 45 feet high in places, with 85 "cubos", semi-circular stone towers. It is 4 miles long. It is quite intimidating to stand in the road outside and look up at it. It is an enjoyable walk – the top of the wall is uneven in places, but quite comfortable to walk on. It dates from the third century and is a magnificent monument to Roman builders.

The town lies on the bank of the River Miño. It has a Celtic foundation, so early Cornish pilgrims would certainly feel a mutual understanding with these people. "Lug" was a Celtic fire god.

In 1129 the building of the Cathedral was begun, on the site of an 8th century building. In mediaeval times, Lugo had five hospitals, so pilgrims were well served.

The pilgrims used one of two gates; they either left the town by the Santiago gate, "Puerto de Santiago", adorned in the 18th century by Santiago Matamoros, or through the Puerto Mino and across the river. The bridge still stands, looking very elegant with its five great pointed arches.

On to Guntin, where we join the old pilgrim route. At Palas del Rey is the Romanesque monastic church of Vilar de Donas. We reach it by a narrow rough lane. The sky is overcast and the light poor. The church is surrounded by trees, which seem to be swallowing it up. It is impossible to get a good view of the exterior because of the trees and an obstructing wall. The doorway is sensitively decorated. We enter; the air is musty and damp, and mould is on floor and walls. A Bible stands on a desk and there is a little pathetic bunch of flowers in a jar. A splendid tomb of a Knight Templar looks out of place. Surely he deserves a more attractive resting place.

We visit Mellid with its long straggling street. Two important churches here, Santa Maria and San Pedro, had hospices attached for accommodating pilgrims.

Santa Maria is a strange church, by a side road, at the end of the town. It is surrounded by small market gardens full of vegetables. The approach is almost blocked by high stone tombs, and at the far end, is a high set of cupboards, each door decorated with ribbon, fading flowers or a branch of yew or cypress. A smiling sacristan opens the door and is delighted by our visit. The floor slopes down; the font has a padlocked cover to prevent the devil from drinking the holy water.

I think the Cornish pilgrims would have felt more at home here than in any other cathedrals or churches I had seen.

Church of Santa Maria, Mellid.

In Search of St. James

Metal doors to receptacles for the dead, decorated with flowers, ribbons and cypress branches. Church of Santa Maria, Mellid.

This granary in Mellid would be familiar to a Cornish country-dweller. It is well protected from rain and sodden earth and the staddle stones on which it stands discourage rats.

The orange-red roof and the trees make an attractive picture.

The hospices in these villages were very necessary, because the journey was nearly over. Many pilgrims needed medical treatment or nursing before continuing on their way. Who would want to give up the struggle now?

From now on we cast our mind forward to our goal. Only a stop now and then to eat a meal or quench our thirst. No more searching for elusive hospices off the beaten track, for soon we shall be entering the city of Santiago de Compostela.

We overtake groups of pilgrims on the road; some young and athletic like the Scouts to whom I talked; some family groups; mainly middle-aged and elderly groups, all purposefully journeying in faith and with a joy in their hearts that is transmitted to all they meet.

Entering a roadside inn for a bar snack, we talk to two pilgrims. One man has come from France. He met his Swiss companion at Burgos, and they journeyed together; sunburnt and travel-stained, with their thick socks and nailed boots, and carrying on their backs a bulging rucksack and in one hand their pilgrim's staff.

We ask them if they will join our group at our own private Mass at 7 a.m. on St. James' Day in the crypt of the Cathedral. They are touched by the invitation but explain that it would be impossible. They show us a roll of paper, rather like a toilet roll. On it was a mass of names. Every village they had passed through recognised them as Pilgrims. People ran to them asking them to pray for a sick child, a bereaved widow, etc. and to all they had pledged that they would offer up all the names at the High Mass. What an example of faith and Christian service.

The Road makes its way along little valleys, at times opening out to give wide horizons, dominated by the Sacro Peak. Soon the mediaeval pilgrims reached Laba-colla where there was a stream of fresh sparkling water.

Fellow-pilgrims: French Scouts (above) and the French pilgrim and his Swiss companion who met at Burgos and travelled on together.

Just what they needed! Many of them stripped and washed "for the love of the Apostle." Here stood a fine cross, but alas on the site is now the airport, so it has been moved into Santiago, in front of the church of San Domingo. Now the groups ran up the Monte del Gozo (Hill of Joy). From the top they could see the towering spires and tower of Santiago. What a moment! All the privations of the journey were forgotten. They had won through at last and could anticipate all the joys to come. The pilgrim who reached the top of the hill first, became the Captain of that particular group.

> "O happy band of Pilgrims
> If onward ye will tread
> With Jesus as your fellow
> With Jesus as your Head"

The sparkling water of Lab-acolla.

I had always sung the words of that hymn rather mechanically. Never again. Now I know what a happy

band of pilgrims is. Now they will soon be wearing the coveted scallop shell.

How did Santiago appear to these pilgrims arriving here for the first time? The pilgrim in mediaeval times felt a compulsion to venture on this long arduous journey to gain assurance of a glorious life after death. By so doing, indulgences would erase the mistakes, backslidings and sins committed in earlier life. On the way many lessons had been learnt. In France, the emphasis seemed to be on pointing out the terrors of hell. The pilgrims would gaze on the tympanum over the door and see magnificent carving portraying the souls of the wicked being prodded with forks, heads being bitten off by ogres, and all surrounded by grinning devils and fabulous animals. This must have been terrifying, but surely succeeded in goading them on to endure dreadful privations – anything to avoid eternal torture and torment. But as the journey progressed the emphasis seemed to change. Less hell and more heaven. Here was hope, and

The park, Santiago.

as the pilgrim gazed up at the tympanum, he was more likely to see an Almighty Father, and help and sanctuary was at hand.

Santiago does not daunt or overwhelm you. It is a small city. You can stand in the park and look out over the green countryside outside. It has not materially changed through the centuries. The Cathedral at the centre is the focal point. The contrasting facades overlook squares of great beauty and interest. Beautiful buildings stand cheek by jowl: you just come upon them, you don't have to search.

The Museum attached to the Cathedral needs days to appreciate thoroughly. The visitor with a roll of tickets,

Santiago. Spanish ladies.

gives up one at a time. First, to see the Spanish
tapestries, full of action and vibrant colour, compared
with the darker and more sombre ones from Belgium.
Then the manuscripts, with their beautiful illumination:
golds and reds and blues in most meticulous work. Here
are great books with music written so large that a whole
choir could use one book. Then, the painting, traced
through the centuries. And many more.

Galicia is unlike the rest of Spain, for the relatively
high rainfall provides a greener landscape and this should
have looked quite familiar to the pilgrims from Ireland,
South Wales and Cornwall. Just the sort of soft weather
they were used to.

Santiago. A priest medi-
tates.

In Search of St. James

In Santiago, one feels that the clock has been put back, and you are visiting a civilization long gone. Here is the least changed remnant of the province of Leon, and its roots stretch back to the days of Visigothic rule.

You would think that the thousands upon thousands of pilgrims to St. James' shrine would have effectively broken this ancient peace. But that is not so. You feel in Santiago, that in spite of all the bustle, excitement, and music from the band and the dancing of the Big Heads, you have only to turn a corner, go through a tunnel or enter a quiet little cafe, and the centuries roll back – the priest strolling through the arcade – the two old Spanish ladies, spotlessly clean, hair combed back into a bun, black shoes, black long skirt and shawl. Silent and timeless.

During the day, the gun, surely as big as Big Bertha, booms to announce that a display, a procession or some other event is about to take place. The band is seated and squeezed into a narrow street, jammed between tables of diners at tables on the pavement. Shoppers crowd the spectacular cake shops, choosing one of this, two of that and three of the other, and either eating them in situ, or carrying them in a beautifully packed circular parcel precariously balanced on one hand. There are little stalls with vendors selling mementoes at the corners of the squares.

Then comes night. With no hurry or commotion, the crowds melt away. The orange light of the setting sun seems to set alight the lichen-covered roofs, and as the light fades, the silhouettes of towers, churches, palaces and monasteries blacken against a grey sky, and the figures on the roof of the Cathedral look even more like chessmen awaiting a move. The light rain falling gives the impression that these buildings are palaces on the seabed, many fathoms deep.

The tense silence can be felt, broken only by chiming clocks and water from the gargoyles splashing onto the stones below.

View of the magnificent
cathedral of Santiago de
Compostela (left) and the
Hotel de los Reyes Catolicos
(below).

The High Altar. Christ is at the centre, attended by hosts of angels. High above stands St. James, wearing his broad-brimmed hat and carrying staff and scrip.

Now let us look at the Cathedral, a fitting climax to the long and hazardous journey.

This magnificent example of religious architecture has acquired its present appearance after centuries of influence from a whole range of architectural styles. Romanesque blends with the most fanciful baroque, and delicate ogival Gothic with the elegance of plateresque.

The Platerias is the oldest facade, most of it contemporary with the interior. It has banked rows of round arches with triple archivolts. It is rich with beautifully carved statues and bas-reliefs.

The Quintana at the crevet of the Cathedral rises gracefully in the shadow of the Berenguela tower. This is a handsome example of Compostelan baroque, designed in the 17th century by Domingo Andrade. The famous Puerta Santa (holy door) is here. This is only opened during Holy Year, that is, when St. James' Day falls on a Sunday. It was in fact Holy Year when I first visited Santiago, so I was privileged to reach the Saint's tomb via this famous door.

The Azabacheria facade comes next, with its confused mixture of styles. Ventura Rodriguez was the architect of some of this work.

Finally, there is the Obradoiro façade, at the head of an imposing flight of steps. It surges up like a huge reredos flanked by the Campanas and Carracas towers. It was designed and built by the brilliant architect Casas y Novoa in the 18th century.

The interior is the supreme masterpiece of Romanesque architecture, embodying all the knowledge and skill of the old mediaeval masters.

On entry, we see the Portico de la Gloria, described by Street in 1869 as "one of the greatest glories of Christian art". Maestro Mateo, who was the sculptor, worked on it from 1166 to 1188, displaying constant freshness and originality. Each figure is lively and unconventional, with details exquisitely refined, as if he did it all himself and left nothing to his assistants. So great was its impact that

The Puerta Santa (Holy Door), Santiago Cathedral.

it was said, "It was here that Daniel's smile heralded the new spirit that was to inspire the art of the Western world."

The central marble shaft is a Jesse tree, its capital, the Trinity, above St. James. The capital above is the Temptation. At the base humbly kneels Mateo. Our Lord is in the centre of the tympanum; around are the Evangelists. Above is a multitude of worshippers. The striking archivolt has the twenty-four Elders. The skill and imagination used in their execution is beyond praise. Its barbaric splendour is wonderfully attractive. The whole triple portico is the Last Judgment, the theme that has followed the Pilgrims along the whole of the Pilgrims' Way from church to church.

This great Romanesque church, built 1075–1128, is related to the pilgrim churches of Tours (which I visited a month ago), Limoges, Conques, Toulouse and Cluny. Its south facade alone is original, so you get a feeling of wholeness; the Pilgrims' Way being a kind of unfolding tapestry with certain threads stretching from starting point to goal and fulfilment.

The three broad, soaring aisles with parabolic arches, the triforium and transepts combine to create an impression of grace and peace. There is no clerestory, but this adds rather than detracts. As you gaze upward from the light reflected from the reredos and side chapels and tombs ablaze with light on the gold and silver, the roof is far off and seemingly unreachable. So, when the Botafumeiro swings to its greatest height, and the sparks fly freely, it is a moment of exhilaration.

The centre of attraction is the body of the Apostle St. James, contained in a silver coffer in a small crypt below the high altar.

The Eve of St. James

The morning breaks warm and sunny. This is unusual. Very often the Festival is celebrated in thick driving rain, reminiscent of a November day at Bolventor. This is the day of rehearsals, of introducing spectators to the strange rites to be the forerunner of the services and processions on the 25th.

Bands practise in the square opposite the Obradoiro facade of the Cathedral, and in front of the local government building.

Then peculiar figures appear. They are grotesque. They have huge heads with leering expressions. They do a square dance. One has a black face, and is probably a Moor, but the significance of the dance is obscure. The children love them. The Big Heads pick them up and carry them about to their evident delight. How different from me. I should have screamed myself into a fit.

To recover from this, we go into the Hotel de Los Reyes Catolicos, on the west side of the square. It was founded as a pilgrims' hospice by Ferdinand and

The Big Heads dance to the delight of the children.

Isabella, after whom it is named. The pilgrims were given every attention, with a bed, food and medical care if necessary. Today it is a Parador, i.e. a 5-star hotel managed by the state. It is a magnificent building, both inside and out. The rooms overlook three cloisters at the back, offering a green tracery of shade.

You don't have to be wealthy to eat here: they cater for all purses. We sit on a stool and drink delicious coffee and munch thin almond biscuits.

Making our way back to the Cathedral, we watch the folk dancers and players assembling round the fountain. These are the finalists who are to compete in the inter-province concert to be held in the evening. How beautiful and graceful the black-haired girls are, and so courteous and good humoured! I particularly like the group from Vigo in their black and red costumes and broad-brimmed hats, carrying oars and fish baskets. I visited Vigo, several years ago, and watched the mussel boats in the bay.

The instrumentalists are men. Their instruments, drums, bagpipes, and strings are typically Celtic and remind me of the Cornish group, who call themselves Bucca. The little bagpiper I speak to is about eight years old: I am glad he isn't blind as were the little bagpipers in mediaeval times.

They go away, probably to have a final rehearsal before the evening concert.

We wander through the arcaded streets, among the throngs of people, manage to find a table on the pavement in front of a cafe, and order a snack and well-earned drink. Along comes the town band, settles down on chairs right across the street, and plays as we eat. All through the celebrations, I see no sign of impatience or irritation. All is harmony.

Back in the Cathedral, the real preparations are being made. Worshippers pass in and out in their thousands. Masses are

sung and said at various altars. There are confessionals

Cheerful folk dancers and musicians.

The band plays in the street, while the audience lunches on the pavement.

ranged down the long aisle, and priests sit in them with curtains drawn back, meditating or reading.

A small boy of about seven years is making his confession, while his mother waits in a pew. He kneels before the priest, who holds his hands between his. They are deep in conversation. Then, suddenly, the boy rises, stands close to the priest and whispers earnestly in his ear. All is understood: the two part with broad smiles.

In the Portico de la Gloria, adults are clasping the pillar in the grooves made by the fingers of pilgrims since mediaeval times, and bowing their heads in prayer in thanks for a safe arrival. I do so as well. Mothers hold tiny children in their arms, so that they can take part in the traditional ritual.

The officials are busy preparing for the solemnities of the festival; vestments for visiting Cardinals and Bishops; a great store of huge candles; the moving of the great wooden statue of Santiago Matamoros, and the

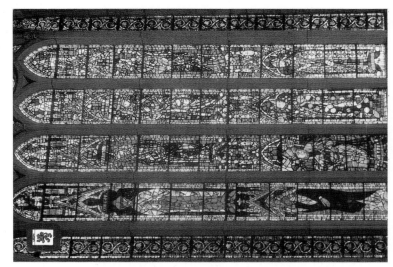

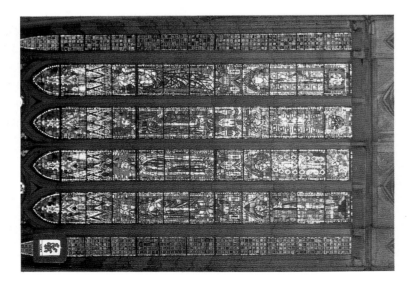

Three of the magnificent
stained glass windows of
Leon Cathedral

XV Xornadas de Folklore Galego

Folk musicians

The Portico de la Gloria. On the central pillar is St. James, holding his pilgrim's staff.

silver and glass case of relics into a transept, and erecting the two thrones for the King and Queen.

"Big Bertha" (only my name for the booming signal gun) sounds, and out from a high door, into the sunlight, come the Giants with their escorts. There is an awed silence, because they really are tremendous. Then everyone applauds.

But there is no time to be lost. We hurry to the square overlooked by the Quintana facade. Staging has been set up, and colourfully dressed dancers are preparing for the concert.

The audience fills the packed rows of seats and waits expectantly. There is no pushing or shouting. Time is of little importance.

At last, the introduction and the spectacle of colour, rhythm and grace moves across the stage. In most dances, the women are statuesque and rhythmic, while the men whirl and leap in complicated patterns. It gives

The Giants cross the Plaza in stately formation.

delight to all, and the applause is tumultuous. At the conclusion, the awards are presented and everyone feels it was the best concert ever.

We go off and have our dinner and a short rest, before the firework display. This is held in the square in front of the Obradoiro facade. Huge set pieces have been erected in front of the Cathedral steps.

We arrive in plenty of time, and we stand and wait. A clear sky and darkness falling. The towers rise black against the sky. All the children are there and mothers and fathers hold the youngsters in their arms, to protect them if the crowd sways and to comfort them when a big banger explodes.

Punctually at 11 p.m. a maroon goes up, red and fiery, and scatters coloured stars against the sky. "Olé", everyone cries.

We see everything in stars, whirling wheels and coloured smoke trails.

The grand finale is a wonderful representation of the cathedral itself.

Everyone claps and behaves as if it had been a symphony concert.

The crowds just melt away – no cars or motorcycles – just feet padding rather wearily towards home.

At about 2 a.m. I hear a metallic clanking as I prepare to retire. I look out of the window. All the refuse bins are being emptied and all the streets and pavements washed in preparation for the great day.

St. James' Day: July 25

In the half light of early morning, each of our group of twenty-one pilgrims rises from a warm bed and peers through the window. Splendid! all the signs give promise of a calm and sunny day. We emerge from our hotel. Everything is silent. We creep along the Calle de Franco into the little Plaza Fonseca. The Berenguela Tower rises above us.

We enter the Cathedral. The absence of a clerestory means that we stumble in the darkness, the hesitant ones trying to follow in the wake of the bolder ones ahead. We come to an iron gate which is unlocked for us, and we descend by an ancient stone staircase to the crypt.

The Dean goes to a vestry to robe, while the candles are lit. We range ourselves with our backs against the stone wall, facing the rails and altar. There are no chairs. We stand or kneel. We are composed and in the right state of mind, when the Dean returns, suitably robed. "Suitably" is perhaps not the right word. Many visiting dignitaries cannot or do not bring their own vestments, and rely on those of the Cathedral, and this works well if you are "off the peg" size. But the Dean is tall, and the dim light contributes to the bizarre figure which appears before us. He must have had the greatest difficulty squeezing into the alb and everything is much too short.

But, when once we have recovered our composure, all that is forgotten, and the Mass is a moving experience.

Even during the service, there are interruptions. Several devout Spanish worshippers, tempted by the open gate, come in; the men clutching caps to their chests, the women wearing black shawls or mantillas. They genuflect and kneel at the rail, but soon realise something is wrong – this is a language strange to them, and so after a few whispers they creep out.

I can still see our collection being taken up on a book, because no bowl or plate is available.

So back to the hotel for breakfast. The weather is perfect, clear and sunny. We are very lucky, because often the feast day turns out to be blustery, cold and wet.

We return to the Cathedral. It is not yet shut. We can see the two thrones set facing the high altar , and the botafumeiro (giant censor) is standing ready to become the climax of the High Mass at 12 noon, to be attended by the King and Queen.

In Search of St. James

We reach the Plaza del Obradoiro, and see a transformation. The Government Building opposite the Cathedral is ablaze with colour. Hanging from the balconies are the huge banners bearing the crests of the various provinces. Protruding from the windows are large flags, pre-eminent among them being the national flag of Spain with its scarlet and gold horizontal stripes.

Brown-uniformed police are everywhere. Rumour has it that there has been a threat to assassinate the King, so police have been drafted in for special duty. The brown uniform is warm and attractive, which matches the men who wear them. They are not coldly efficient; they are quite relaxed and stroll about in groups among the people.

The city officials emerge at intervals, looking quite smart in morning suits.

The army is represented by a small column about 50 strong.

Everyone is delighted that the King and Queen are on their way. Yesterday there were fears that substitutes would be sent. But all is well. They have cut short their visit to South America, to attend High Mass here.

A helicopter flies overhead, bringing news from the nearby airport.

Suddenly, the police realise that all is not well. The King and Queen are expected to arrive in about an hour, and the Plaza is packed to capacity with people. No-one had thought to rail off an area to allow them access. Up to now the hordes of police had done nothing but lounge about and fraternise with the natives! Now that must stop. They must put on a stern front, and show who are masters. Senior officers begin to shout, and police start pushing the people back across the Plaza. But of course, there isn't any space at the back for them to occupy. Indignant shouts, as spectators see their vantage point being usurped, and agonized yells as feet are trampled on. Never mind – ten yards' progress has been made, so the police relax. Several of them manage to get surrep-

The Plaza is packed to capacity with people.

titious puffs of their cigarettes, by changing hands and breathing out over their shoulders. Then comes another onslaught – and so on. The police do not achieve their objective, but seemingly do not expect to. Small children keep appearing between the legs of the front row, as the tide sweeps over them. When the tide sweeps back, the re-emerged are identified, and sit on the ground, miraculously still in one piece.

Aristocratic limousines arrive and depart at irregular intervals. There are several false alarums, which galvanise the soldiers and City Elders to stand to attention, until when the right cars do arrive they are nearly caught unawares.

At long last, the Royal party appears and goes into the City Hall. The procession begins to form and the two bands begin to play. Then comes the short walk to the Cathedral. I am lucky and have a good vantage point.

First the Guard has to be inspected. Caps and tunics

are neat, but Oh! the shoes. They need polish. Perhaps it is this defect that causes embarrassment and causes them to march out of step.

The procession is headed by magnificent flags and two heralds, who look exactly like Jacks in playing cards. They wear square hats, white ruffs, tunics, breeches, white stockings and black shoes. Their attendants look like Gentlemen-at-Arms; one group wears red and white plumes, the other green and white.

The King wears morning dress and is hatless. I am glad he wears no uniform. The Queen wears a white silk dress, with black Spanish embroidery down one side.

The King waves and smiles. There is no frenzied shouting, just warm applause.

As the clocks strike the hour, the procession enters the Cathedral. The Archbishop is at the door to welcome them, and when the King and Queen are seated, the Mass begins.

The Cardinals and Bishops, in all shades of reds and pinks, make a dazzling display. The music is impressive, and the choir obviously enjoys singing, but, again in the

The King and Queen with escort enter the cathedral.

61

Spanish tradition, attention to detail is not all it might be.

When the King stands to speak, there is absolute silence, and he speaks with great conviction and emphasis.

The climax of the service is the swinging of the Botafumeiro. Six men in scarlet cassocks stand around it, as it stands at the crossing of the transepts. The incense is lighted, the men hold a rope each, and by carrying out a rhythmic pulling and relaxing, the censor begins to swing north-south in ever increasing arcs. The incense blazes and sparks fly windly around. When it almost reaches the roof, the tempo slackens, and the excitement is over.

I have been told that in mediaeval times, poor, wretched, and sick pilgrims were laid on straw above the transept, so that they could see the elevation of the Host, and the smoke could fumigate the air.

When the service is ended, dignitaries are presented to the King. They think our Dean is a Bishop, so he is in the line, still looking somewhat constrained by his vestments.

Now for the final celebration: the procession through the City and the blessing of the Archbishop.

It takes the rest of the afternoon to prepare for it. This is where the old men show their skill and experience. In the transept near the Platerias door is a hive of activity. A great wooden statue showing Santiago Matamoros has to be carried with thick poles resting on young men's shoulders. This used to be always done by butchers, because of their muscles, but no longer. So you see the old men sitting around, giving advice.

Our Lady is on a platform, and has to be decorated with flowers. She is to be carried also, so everything must be firmly fixed. I can't watch this, because any undue swaying or spilling of flowers has to be rectified with hammer and nails.

Candles are unpacked and distributed. They are fat, of yellow wax, and about two feet long.

The Botafumeiro.

The Procession

The great doors are open, and the Crucifer appears flanked by acolytes with lanterns on poles.

This is followed by the great statue of Matamoros. Already, you can see the strain and apprehension on the bearers' faces, as they stumble down the ten steps. The choristers follow in white albs with their music.

The Archbishop of Santiago, in mitre and cope with the Cardinals and flanked by Bishops, walks majestically in procession.

The relics, carried in a beautiful silver casket.

The Choir and the Procession

The Procession is the climax of the whole pilgrimage.

Our Lady surrounded by white flowers, which haven't a chance of spilling to the ground, is followed by a beautiful glass and silver casket containing the relics. Then come the local government officials in morning dress. As they wend their way though the streets, the choir sings.

The people congregate in the Plaza Obradoiro to see the procession return to the Cathedral and climb the winding staircase.

Suddenly the six black-faced giants appear. They cross the square and form a guard of honour for the procession to show the submission of the Moors to the Christians. It is very dramatic.

Now comes the winding twisted staircase which has to be negotiated, and it is a great test of strength and skill. But all is well. Perspiration running down their faces, the bearers are triumphant.

As a result of the weather and many hot hands, the candles have assumed all kinds of peculiar shapes, but when they are lit in the Cathedral, it will make a fitting ending to a wonderful day.

The Archbishop, from the top of the steps, says a prayer and calls down a blessing on the people, on the city, and on the world.

PAX VOBISCUM

My pilgrimage is over, but will never be forgotten. It has illuminated my life.

Now, as the excitement subsides, we begin to plan our journey home.

We drive north to Finisterre. The rain shrouds the countryside. Truly, Galicia on a day like this reminds me of a depression over Cornwall, and the stone walls dividing the fields are rather like Cornish hedges, or perhaps more like those in Ireland. Ours are more professional.

In Search of St. James

We drive for a day in Asturias, the weather still bleak and wet. Perhaps the inclement weather was one reason why this was the only part of Spain which was unconquered by the Moors.

We visit a large Celtic village at Poblado, on a hillside. It has only recently been unearthed. It is very like Chysauster.

We drive to Covadonga, where the beautiful high pointed bridge has a cross hanging from the arch. We visit the ravine where the Moors suffered their first defeat. A little chapel has been excavated from the rocky wall.

After a rather hair-raising drive through the Picos de Europe, we travel on to Santander to board a plane for Heathrow and home.

What an experience it had been! I had followed the Pilgrims' Way as nearly as possible, and that in itself was moving and impressive.

I had seen a wealth of architectural wonder and fabulous treasure, which was the outpouring of a faith which helped to produce the sublime. The rigours the pilgrims endured with stoicism, I can now begin to appreciate.

And the goal made everything worth while. I am proud to be able to number myself with the Cornish pilgrims who travelled on the Great Pilgrimage to Santiago de Compostela in those far off days of the Middle Ages.

BIBLIOGRAPHY

The Episcopal Registers of Walter Bronescombe, Diocese of Exeter 1257–1307. Peter Quivil 1293–1307 by the Rev. F.C. Hingston-Randolph M.A. Prebendary of Exeter 1889.

Medieval Cornwall by L.E. Elliott Binns. D.D. 1955. Methuen & Co. Ltd. London.

The Encyclopedia Britannica. 14th Edition.

Lake's Parochial History of the County of Cornwall I 1867. II 1870 Joseph Polsue. Published in Truro.

Ports and harbours of Cornwall. Richard Pearse. Published St. Austell. H.E. Warne 1963.

Devon & Cornwall. Record Society.

New Series Vol. 21.

A calendar of Early Chancery Proceedings relating to West Country Shipping 1388–1493. 1976. Edited and with an introduction by Dorothy M. Gardiner.

A history of the Parish and church of Kilkhampton 1926. Rev. R. Dew. M.A. Rector of Kilkhampton. London. Wells, Gardner, Darton & Co. Ltd.

Hencken; Hugh O'Neill – Archeology of Cornwall & Scilly. 1932. London, Methuen.

The Ecclesiastical History of West Cornwall. By Charles Henderson. R.I.C. (N.S) Vol II pt 3 1955. Pt 4 1956. Vol III Pt 2 1956. Pt 4 1960.

Essays in Cornish History by the same author. 1935. Oxford at the Clarendon Press.

Carew's Survey of Cornwall. Richard Carew of Antony 1555–1620. Edited and with an introduction by F.E. Halliday 1953.

Holy Wells of Cornwall by A. Lane Davies. Published by Federation of Old Cornwall Societies 1970.

The Life of S. Nectan 12th century. Translation by Gilbert Hunter Doble from the M.S. discovered in the Ducal Library at Gotha. 1940. Published Torquay Devonshire Press; Cornish Saints series No. 45.

The Story of Fowey (Cornwall) by John Keast. 1950. Printed by James Townsend & Sons Ltd. Exeter.

An introduction to the Archaeology of Cornwall by Charles Woolf. 1970. Published by D. Bradford Barton Ltd.

The Holy Wells of Cornwall. J.F. Meyrick. 1982. Published by the author. Printed by the Falmouth Printing Co. Ltd.

The Patent Roll and Bishop John de Grandison's Register. 1327–1369 by the Rev. F.C. Hingeston-Randolph. M.A. 1889.

Pilgrim Life in the Middle Ages. 1911 by Sidney Heath. Published by T. Fisher Unwin, London.

England in the Late Middle Ages by A.R. Myers. 1969 Published by Penguin.

Perilous Pilgrimage by Irene Northam.

The Pilgrimage to Santiago. Edwin Mullins. Seckers Warburg. 1974.

The Great Pilgrimage of the Middle Ages. Vera and Helmut Hell.

St. James in Spain. Sir Thomas Kendrick. 1960 Methuen.

The Cathedrals of Spain. John Harvey. 1957 Batsford.